Sister a

Blessings to You
+ Your Husband +
Family!

The Celestial Advantage

Thank You for
Your Support!

Your Brother

Overseer Pastor
OEH!

The Celestial Advantage
Obadiah E. Harris

ISBN: 978-1-950719-08-2 (Paperback)
ISBN: 978-1-950719-09-9 (eBook)

Any references to historical events, real people, or real places are used fictitiously. Names, characters, and places are products of the author's imagination.

First printing edition 2019.

J Merrill Publishing, Inc.
434 Hillpine Drive
Columbus, OH 43207

www.JMerrillPublishingInc.com

Dedication

ALL GLORY TO GOD WHO INSPIRES MY WRITING DESIRES!

I want to dedicate, "The Celestial Advantage" to my Lovely Wife, Karen Ann Harris!

Karen, your Love, Devotion, and Support have enhanced my creativity for Spiritual possibilities!

Also, Jackie Smith Jr.; Yes, JMSJ, for EVERYTHING you do... I Appreciate You!

Blessings OEH

In our Angel, intensified battles of life, with strife potentially pulverizing you through things both seen and unseen, we must be aware of "The Celestial Advantage." This term may be new to your vocabulary, or everyday vernacular, but the concept is totally "GOD PROLIFIC." That when the child of GOD is totally outmanned, in a deficit, or deficient imposition, in his human position, that GOD will totally swing the pendulum of domination in his favor through a Celestial, or Angelic Intervention.

Let us consider Elisha in 2 Kings the 6th chapter when he is surrounded by the Syrians with their troops, horses, and chariots everywhere, and the servant of the man of GOD asked, "Alas my master! How shall we do? "Yes, what shall we do? But Elisha with his transcendent spiritual vision saw GOD's Incomparable provision, "And he answered, Fear not: for they that be with us are more than they that be with them" Then Elisha prayed, and said, LORD, I pray thee, open his eyes, that he may see. And THE LORD opened the eyes of the young man, and he saw: and behold, the mountain was full of horses and chariots of fire round about Elisha.

Elisha had the "Vision and Provision" because GOD had given him "The Celestial Advantage".

In modern times 4 out of 5 Americans say that they believe in GOD, whereas 56% believe in The One True God of the Bible. One poll of Religious investigators calculated that 77%

of Americans believed in Angels, with 88% of Christians being in that numerical categorization, but man opinionates, speculates and investigates, but GOD is the All-knowing Authority of the Truth, and we must know the truth, and the truth will set us free.

Saints and Friends as we enter into dialogue to excavate the Biblical Goldmine of scriptural verification for yourself, as I say profusely, man has his opinion but, God has dominion. So, never play Russian roulette with Bible passages because, if we add anything to it God will add unto us the plagues that are in The Book and, if we subtract anything out of it, He will remove our name from the Book of Life (Revelation 22:19).

But, in an age of racism, phony-ism, cronyism, and parochialism, be meticulous and never ridiculous in your reverential approach with all men. Xenophobes, or those having hatred, bigotry, animosity, or being fearful of strangers, Hebrews 13:2 declares, "Be not forgetful to entertain strangers: for thereby some have entertained angels unawares."

But to balance the prevailing scales of discerning accuracy read 2 Corinthians 11:11 because it reveals that "Satan" can transform himself into an "angel of light" and that this 'sinister minister' can also charade, masquerade, or insinuate himself in camouflage into the body of Christ "...whose end shall be according to their works," 2 Corinthians 22:15

Know this that the Law of 1st Mention is a Revelation of the Divine scriptural purpose of intentionality, and deposited in the first Biblical interview of introduction is a portrait that will magnify, multiply in supernatural supply the most veritable book ever written, which is the Bible.

After Adam and Eve sinned, the tree of life which before was accessible to them was now by divine command emphatically prohibited lest they eat of it and live forever in their sinful condition. And, how horrific it is to contemplate the eternal spiritual death that would be perpetuated every time another child of degeneracy would be birthed into this post fall catastrophe.

So God in Genesis 3:24, yes we see, So he drove out the man; and he placed at the east of the garden of Eden Cherubim's, and a flaming sword which turned every way, to keep the way of the tree of life."

When God 'drove' man out of the garden, it was not by preferred chauffeur limousine luxuriation But, 'drove' in the Hebrew is the word 'garash' meaning to drive out, expel, cast out, thrust out, or divorce.

It was an enforced eviction from a property that he no longer could claim residency. A loss of title deed or ownership because of the sinfully destitute condition that he had by his own decision to please himself, and it was enforced through a divinely appointed Cherubim who protected the tree of life along with a 'flaming sword which turned every way.'

The cherubim were angels that not only were guardians of Eden and were residential to the presence of God's throne room but, also were hovering artistically over the Ark of the Covenant.

How awesome with the revelation that these four-faced celestials with the face of a man, an ox, a lion, and an eagle would not only guard God's holiness but prevent man from further destroying himself. Could it be that the greatest enemy that an angel protects you from is you! With the face of a man, an angel could look face to face with a man and understand his human demands and carry them out through God's divine commands.

In Romans 13:14 there is a God-ordained structure for a divinely orchestrated order of obedience, and it states that the minister of God is not a threat to those that are good but, rather to evildoers.

So angels...are they not ministering spirits sent forth to minister for them who shall be heirs of salvation.

Yes, angels are for them and you. If salvation is your goal, then your angels help minister to keep your life under control.

It is the prayerful, meditative, contemplative focus on God that activates the celestial band on the ladder of God's vision of success to help humanity be the best that he can be. Yes, humankind is not always kind in his vigorous determinations to reach strategic life exalted destinations. Yes, and he will sometimes bring his denominations into his religious affiliations to achieve his persuasions of greatness.

So here is Jacob, whose name characterized his underhanded methodologies. Yes, 'the heel catcher' after exploiting his father Isaac and his brother Esau to receive the patriarchal blessing in pursuit of life like a paradise. But, after that, running for his life to avoid a catastrophic ending. To some who will without reservation thieve to achieve, the paradise that is like treacherous gambling, yes, a roll of a pair of dice in which they will gamble their soul and gain the world but lose their soul.

But, Jacob's deceptions were intercepted with a dynamic revelation encounter with God that still leaps from the pages of the Bible with exceeding joy and a vertical leap that is immeasurable.

This paradigm shift, this electrifying epiphany, fully comprehended will change the definition of 'climbing the ladder of success.' Whether from an individualistic viewpoint of calibrating, or calculating the path of promotion, that sometimes in a corporate world demands that a carnivorous shark-like meat eating disposition be actively engaged to gobble up the competition and wipe out the vicious rivals of earthly success.

But here Jacob took some 'stones' and made a pillow. Yes, 'stones' that gave a relational picture of the constitutional nature of Jesus Christ who was THE Stone, The Petra (Matthew 16:18) of stability, the immovable stone. Yes, the rock of ages. As Jacob rested his head, in harmonious heavenly synchronization, yes spiritual symphony between Jacob, God, the angels and eternity was achieved. As he dreamed, there was a vision of a 'ladder' the Hebrew word 'cullam' (pronounced "su-lam") that reached from the earth and the top of it to Heaven. The ladder with its rungs of progressive levels of higher altitudes, yes, higher than the 'lithosphere (land), hydrosphere (water), biosphere (living things) and the atmosphere and into the throne room where God reigns at the top! And the angels of God were ascending and descending" upon this 'ladder of success. Therefore this place was called Bethel, which was defined as the" The House of God, and The gate of Heaven. As we enter into submissive rest with God and solitary meditative oneness with Him, watch Him dispatch His angels with unanimous celestial activities in our lives as God stands at the top of the ladder of eternal success. Although in visualization we may not see them, except, by way of discernment, we must know that As Hebrews 1:14 reveals "Are they not all ministering spirits, sent forth to minister for them Who shall be heirs of salvation?" Oh yes if cataracts, or the visionary cloud or optical limitations were removed from our eyes, then we would see the celestial bands, operating at God's Commands, to satisfy our earthly demands.

Major Ideas Summary

A subject evoking or provoking much elaboration and theological speculation is "the help" provided by God's angelic attendants.

The term "Angel" originates from the Greek term "angelos," which in its simplistic presentation refers to a messenger or one who is sent and therefore simplistically is equated to a majestic mailman that prevails for man. Though these beings of celestial origination are described as supernatural agents of change, the prestigious nature of their operations is revealed in the fact that God created them. Their status receives further elevation in the fact that the term "angelos" is associated with our modern word "evangelism" therefore, the implication of the word association is that "Angels" are God's messengers sent with "good news", since evangelize defines the activity of a person sent with "good news".

Among the Jewish community of ancient times, it was foregone conclusion concerning the help provided by angels, they (the Jews) prescribed to the premise that 200 angels controlled the stars, while one exclusively preeminent angel called the "calendar angel supremely presided over the never-ending succession of days, months and years. Some supposed angelic experts believed that a mighty angel took care of the stars, while simultaneously others were presiding over the frost, the dew, the rain, the snow, the hail, the thunder, and the lightning. One rabbi's doctrinal extravagance led him to surmise that every blade of grass had an angelic overseer.

The Hebrew world also adhered to the belief that some angels were assigned to the responsibilities of the dead, while others were specified to oversee the affairs of nations or the diverse races of people.

They also doctrinalized that seven angels were especially elect and that in this higher categorization was Michael, Raphael, and Gabriel. They concluded that Michael's sphere was the vindication of God that Raphael was the angel of bodily cures and that Gabriel was in charge of special revelations.

Even in ancient Egyptology, there are legendary tales of angelic facilitation in their geographical location. Louis Golding in his book "In the steps of Moses: elaborated on such a legend, stating that the baby Moses, rescued from the Nile River, removed the crown from Pharaoh's head then placed it on his own head. The story reports that this was considered such an evil omen and a potential threat to the throne, that a council meeting convened to determine what shall we do? The decision according to the legend states, two platters were placed before the child. One contained "jewels" and the other "live coals." The story declares that the baby reached for the jewels, but that the angel Gabriel thrust his hand sideways toward the live coals. Then, he (Moses) lifted them, burning his tongue and lips, and therefore was spared from the pharaoh believing that he was an ultimate threat to the throne (please note the angelic prominence in the legend). But truly as we search for different views in our educational, and academic understanding, the only philosophies that stand the test, are those that are verified through scriptural accuracy.

In the book of Hebrews 1:14 the writer discourses concerning the angelic assistance to the believer by declaring, "Are they not all ministering spirits, sent forth to minister for them who shall be heirs of salvation." The Greek term "leitourgikos" is employed to articulate the job description of "ministering spirits." This term "leitourgikos" describing the helpful angelic advantage to the child of God was utilized in the Septuagint to describe Aaron and his sons" responsibilities (Exodus 31:10) "to minister" in the priest's office.

In I Corinthians 4:9, Paul enlarges upon the angelic activities, as he describes the human events as being under angelic surveillance by declaring, "for we are made a spectacle... to angels." The term spectacle is the word "theatron" associated with our modernistic word "theater," but it by no means implies that human activities are merely a spectator sport of observation among the angels. The word spectacle has been connectively linked with the Roman general's victorious procession that was called a "triumph," in which the general would showcase his great victory, openly displaying his prisoners in chains, including the conquered king. Imagine the celebratory ambiance among angels, who rejoice at the salvation victory accomplishments of God's children.

In Genesis 21, there is prototypically recorded angelic assistance and provision in the life of Ishmael, the son of Abraham and Hagar, Sara's handmaiden. Ishmael whose name means "God heareth" was excommunicated from the Abrahamic household along with Hagar, his mother, through the influence of Sara. Though Ishmael and Hagar were given bread and a bottle of water, soon the supplies dissipated in the desert environment. But then, God heard the voice of the lad, and the "angel of God" called to Hagar out of heaven, and said unto her, what aileth thee, Hagar? Fear not; for God hath heard the voice of the lad, and hold him in thine hand; for I will make him a great nation. And God opened her eyes, and she saw a well of water; and she went, and filled the bottle with water, and gave the lad todrink (Genesis 21:17-19). Certainly, the "angel of God's help is indispensably important in the preservation of Ishmael, and Hagar.

In John 5:3-4, there is documented the healing agency that took place at the pool of Bethesda, "a great multitude of impotent folk, of blind, halt, withered, waiting for the moving of water. For an angel went down at a certain season into the pool, and troubled the water: whosoever then first after the troubling of the water stepped in was made whole of whatsoever disease he had".

Angelic intervention also played a major role in the life of Elijah, who though he had experienced a very dramatic victory over the prophets of Baal, he was still devastated by the threats of Jezebel. After running many miles, finally, he sat down under a juniper tree and gave up stating, "O Lord take away my life; for I am not better than my fathers (1 Kings 19:4)

But then in a great contributory manner to Elijah's emotional, physical, spiritual and psychological restoration, "an angel touched him, and said unto him, arise and eat. And he looked, and behold there was a cake baking on the coals, and cruse of water at his head. And he did eat and drink, and laid him down again. And the angel of the Lord came again the second time, and touched him, and said, arise and eat; because the journey is too great for thee. And he arose, and did eat and drink, and went in the strength of that meat forty days and forty nights unto Horeb the mount of God" (1 Kings 19:5-8).

After Jesus, our Saviour, decisively won the three-dimensional wilderness temptation from the devil, he was so physically hungry and exhausted that the "Angels (of God) came and ministered unto him (Matthew 4:11) 8 in this instance, the term "ministered is diakoneo", meaning to serve, to wait upon, or be an attendant.

A point of indisputable reality is the power and reality of Satan. The term Satan is derived from the Greek term "satanas," meaning "an adversary." This term appears 36 times in the New Testament and has been taken directly from the Hebrew language where it describes a traitor (1Kings 11:23-25), an adversary (Zech. 3:1) and the tempter who audaciously moves David to number Israel.

This historical figure and notorious enemy of God and mankind is also referred to as the "devil." The appellation, or designation the "devil" adds evidence to the demoralized nature of this being, since the term "devil is translated from "diabolos" meaning "one who throws between, and is modernized in the present vernacular as "throwing a monkey wrench in the works."

The Hebrew disdain for this evil personality is established with a greater magnitude when Satan is referred to as Beelzebul. Original the form of this modified word was Baalzebub, which was a pagan Canaanite deity meaning "lord of the flies. "But the Jews in utter disrespect and contempt applied this epithet to Satan.

This creature that is the enemy of all that is righteous was originally created by God to be "Lucifer," an angel of light, and anointed cherub for God's glory. Many believe that "Lucifer," whom the Bible declares "You had the seal of perfection, full of wisdom and perfect in beauty was the ruling prince of the universe under God until his rebellious insurrection.

Ezekiel 28:11-19 provides pertinent and insightful information concerning a historical figure, the king of Tyrus, who was a typical presentation of Lucifer.

God in His analysis of Lucifer's pre-sin deformation status declares..."You were the anointed cherub who covers, and I placed you there. You were on the holy mountain of God. You walked amid the stones of fire. You were blameless in all your ways from the day you were created until unrighteousness was found in you".

Isaiah presents additional explanatory details concerning Lucifer's celestial fall, as Isaiah 14:13-17 states his egomaniacal aspirations through his "I wills." I will ascend into heaven; I will exalt my throne above the stars of God, I will sit also upon the mount of the congregation, I will ascend above the heights of the clouds. I will be like the most high." Truly the ruination of Lucifer's angelic purity was orchestrated by his megalomaniac and singular focus of concentricity. I, I, I. Then in addition to his nonsensical personal rebellion, Revelation 12:4-9 reveals that his heavenly expulsion was accompanied by . . ." the third part of the stars (angels) of heaven. "Though this being is indisputably powerful, God established a pattern of victory over this adversary, that will continue through Armageddon, the last war of human history when Christ and His armies will apply a quietus like victory over the devil once and for all. And this will eventuate in his being cast unto the "Lake of fire"...

Many believe that Lucifer ruled universally during the pre-Adamite era and that when he sinned the world was wrecked with chaotic consequential upheaval, through violent water convulsions of such overwhelming proportions that every living creature was destroyed.

It is also conjectured that his sin defection caused darkness to emerge while causing the sun, the moon, and the stars to lose their properties of luminosity. Those philosophical components of the belief state also that the earth degenerated into a vegetationally dead planet, forced into the winter of its existence, by being submerged in waters that congealed into ice, and possibly being the causative fatality behind the archaeological discovery of many immense quadrupeds and winged creatures. Obviously, something detrimental to God's creatorial excellence occurred since Isaiah 45:18 reveals, "Thus saith the Lord that created the heavens, He is God: that formed the earth and made it; He established it, He created it not a waste, He formed it to be inhabited.

As a result of his fall Lucifer who was an angel of musical prominence, since the Bible declares that "the service of the tabrets and thy pipes was with thee on the day when thou wast created," became the devil.

Though this evil personality is powerful, he is not omnipotent as is indicated by his mandatory activities of accountability before God, in Job 1:7 and 2:2-13 the passage presents the angels appearing at Divinely predetermined times before God. . . "and that Satan always appeared with them." When the Lord said to Satan, "Whence comest thou? He then replied, "From going to and fro in the earth and from walking up and down it." In 1 Peter 5:8, there is more evidential proof that the present deleterious intentions of the devil involve the earthly domain, since our, " adversary the devil, as a roaring lion, walketh about, seeking whom he may devour." The term "devour" crystallizes the purpose of Satan, since the term is the Greek word "katapino" meaning to drink down, and is translated as "to swallow," or drowned" elsewhere.

The activities of the devil, though indiscriminately evil are vastly expansive. He is called the "prince of the power of the air, the spirit that now worketh in the children of disobedience." The phraseology "prince" of the power of the air" probably refers to Satan's present authority over the host of demons who exist in the heavenly sphere. The term "prince" is "archon" which presents this evil figure as the ruler behind the pervasively evil world system", His present influential exertion over the "children of disobedience" is explicated in the fact that "disobedience" is "apeitheia", meaning "the condition of being unpersuadable", while denoting obstinacy, or the obstinate rejection of the will of God.

This demoralized "devil," which means accuser or slanderer accuses the saints before God and slanders the characters of God before men. Though, as already forestated the "devil" in the Greek means "diabolos," but in the Hebrew, the etymon is "sair" meaning a hairy goat, or a he-goat. In direct contradistinction to their sheep cousins, goats are independent, willful, curious, and are typically presented as objects of irresponsible leadership. Biblically the "sair" spirit symphonizes with the devil since the he-goat is a symbol of all that is low and base. It is interesting to note that this designation has a secondary meaning which is a spoiler, or one whose touch soils and besmirches and rearranges.

In Revelation 9:11, Satan is presented as "Abaddon, or Apollyon" which links together the Greek and Hebrew names, which means destroyer. In his activities in this capacity, he is a destructionist, the king of the abyss or bottomless pit. Also in Revelation 12:3-4, 7, 9, etc. he is also called "dragon," which in the Greek language is "drakon" denoting a mythical monster, a large serpent, designated as such because of his keen power of sight. In the Hebrew "the dragon" is tannoth," meaning a howler, a jackal, or one who makes a noise like a howling jackal in the wilderness while enforcing the dangerous character of him who seeks our destruction.

Therefore, with such an evil character on the loose, the Holy Ghost believer must, "Put on the whole armour of God, that ye may be able to stand against the wiles of the devil (Ephesians 6:11).

The term "stand against: is the word "histemi," which was utilized in a militaristic connotation to convey the idea of holding a critical position while under attack (from the devil). The devil's manner of destructive attack is revealed through the term wiles. Wiles is derived from the original word "methodia," from which our English word "method" originates. The term "methodia" was employed with regularity to explain the activities of the wild animal who cunningly stalked and then used stealth, or the element of surprise to pounce on its prey.

In II Corinthians 4:4, the devil is revealed as, "the god of this world hath blinded the minds of them which believe not, lest the light of the glorious gospel of Christ who is the image of God, should shine unto them." The term for "blinded" is tuphloo," meaning to burn, or to smoke. Imagine the distorted effects of a mind (noema), meaning thought, or design which being "blinded," now has an intellect that is satanically dulled, preventing the gospel reception.

In St. John 8:39, Jesus engaged in a spiritual heritage determination discussion with the Jews who declared..."Abraham is our father". But Jesus responded by telling his spiritually unregenerate audience that "So ye are of your father the devil, and his works you will do. He was a murderer from the beginning. And abode not in the truth, because there is no truth in him. When he speaketh a lie, he speaketh of his own: for he is a liar and the father of it".

When Jesus places his ungodly opponents under the devil's fatherhood, He utilizes the term "pater." A word connected with our English words paternity, meaning to become a father. Yes, a paternalism which illustrates the fatherly care exercised by governments for those whom they govern, while placing the individual under the patriarchal control of a father who operates over his house, or family.

Veritably to the unregenerate who are under the "pater, paternity, or paternalism of the devil, it is a most horrendous association since their father is "The thief...that...cometh not but for to steal, and, kill and to destroy...but in a gloriously advantageous contrast, Jesus states...I am come that they might have life and that they might have it more abundantly".

Even the Divine assessment of the devil being "The Thief"...that's come to steal, reveals his criminality since the word steal is "klepto," which characterizes the devil as a "kleptomaniac."

Second Corinthians 11:3 reveals the devil's method in Eve's spiritual defection as "subtility" (Greek panourgia"), which literally means "all working," doing everything in relation to "unscrupulous conduct," or craftiness.

In relation to the devil's activity as the "prince of the power of the air," this by no means restricts his diabolical workings to the 80 or 100 miles of atmosphere that supposedly surrounds the earth. Some have speculated that this evil being's limited power extends to the sun, or to the whole solar system, which would include the immense space in which the planets or our galaxy revolve. There is an idolatrous association between Satan and the universal error of the worship of the sun-god. Sun worship has been observed heathenistically through diverse denominations such as San, Shamas, Bel, Ra, Baal, Moloch, Milcom, Hada, Adrammelech, Mithras, Apollo, Sheik Shems, etc. It is particularly noteworthy the name Satan is translated in Chaldaic equivalence as Sheltan, and into the Greek as Titan, which was utilized by the Greek and the Latin poets as a designation of the Sun-god.

But most important is the fact that "Christ" achieved a victory at Calvary that defeated the devil once and for all, wresting the scepter of authority from him, and Christ is Lord over all.

Another point of major Theological gravity is revealed in the fact of the existence of "Angelic Organization." In medieval times theologians believed that the angelic ranks of organizational gradations were divided into ten categorizations some believe a possible synopsis of the divisions would include archangels, angels, seraphim, cherubim, principalities, authorities, powers, thrones, might, and dominion.

In defining "arch angels" the term in the original Greek is "arch angelos." The word "arch" meaning "chief" principal, or great angel provides self-explanatory insight into the archangel's preeminent stature in the angelic hierarchy stratifications of power.

In the Biblical passages, the archangel Michael's angelic prominence is so spectacularly effective that he has been designated by commentators the Prime Minister in God's administration of the universe.

Though Michael's exploits have received much literary and conversational attention, his recognition of his subservient capacity to God is forever before us, since the name means "who is like God."

In Daniel's book titled after the similitude of his name is to provide the prima facie, or the introductory view of Michael and his God commissioned responsibilities. It was during the third year of Cyrus King of Persia (Daniel 10:1), that Daniel prayed, "from the first day... thy words were heard", but an oppositional force called the prince of the Kingdom of Persia withstood him 21 days (Daniel 10:12-13). But then Michael true to the reality of his name "who is like God,"...being...one of the chief princes came to help...

In Revelation 12:7-12, Michael and his angels triumphantly defeat Satan and his armies in the battle of the ages.

It is of great importance to the rapture conscious child of God, that at the Second Coming of Jesus the voice of an "archangel," undoubtedly Michael's will precede the miraculous procession of the resurrection of the saints and their heavenly transfer.

Another angel whose name receives universal recognition and visibility of acclamation is "Gabriel," whose name means "God's hero," Emery H. Bancroft in his book on Christian Theology presents the premise of an individual believing Gabriel to be an archangel.

Gabriel whose name may also mean "the mighty one or God is great," Is the angelic figure that emerges to divulge the purposes and verdicts of the plan of God, and who also provided a panoramic view of the successive earthly kingdoms, before Christ Jesus' return.

In the holiest scriptures, Gabriel is mentioned four times. In Daniel 8:6, 9:21, and Luke 1:19 and Luke 1:26.

In Daniel chapter 9 Gabriel is so accurately in tune with the eschatological Messianic fulfillment, that he appears to Daniel providing him with the exact time required to rebuild and restore Jerusalem (49 years) and then the remaining time elapsed for the Christological sacrifice for mankind (434 years.

In St. Luke 1:5-38, there is recorded two Gabriel visitations to communicate essential Messianic details. First, he appears to the priest Zacharias announcing the birth of John the Baptist (his son) who in verse 17, "shall go before Him in the spirit and power of Elias, to turn the hearts of the fathers to the children and the disobedient to the wisdom of the just; to make ready a people prepared for the Lord.

Then Gabriel appeared to Mary, a virgin who was engaged to a Davidic descendant called Joseph, foretelling that she would be the mother of the Saviour, without sexual cohabitation, as the "power of the Most High" (God) overshadowed her (Luke 1:34).

Another group of angels operating in the Divine service is the "Seraphim," which has been interpreted as meaning "love, nobles, or the burning ones." Some propose that the definition "burning ones" is illustrative of their burning devotion to God from the hearts that are ablaze to worship Him.

In Isaiah 6, the Seraphim angels are introduced as six-winged beings. While their operations were dominated by a God worshipping concentricity, since "with two wings he covered his face and with two he covered his feet." Then it was with the additional two wings that he did fly".

It is therefore of little surprise that the Bible, with great clarity, expresses the Seraphim declarations or articulations, which is holy, holy, holy is the Lord of hosts the whole earth is full of His glory".

The passage of Isaiah chapter 6, while being a testimony to the awesome holiness of God, also brings into full view the inadequacies of a man whose sinful disposition is accentuated in the dawning reality of the presence of God. Therefore, Isaiah, being greatly overwhelmed by God's glory declared, "Woe is me! For I am undone; because I am a man of unclean lips and I dwell in the midst of a people of unclean lips: for mine eyes have seen the king, the Lord of hosts."

Then with such a confession of personal condescension, the Seraphim with great reactionary effectiveness removes burning coals from the altar, then touches Isaiah's lips while cleansing his iniquity and purging his sin. Therefore, with such a dynamic, productive touch, Isaiah enthusiastically declares, "Here am I; send me."

In relation to the six wings, it is of the utmost importance that the Seraphim duties express the need for the predominance of worship in serving God. Since two wings were employed to cover his feet, yes to protect God's holiness and two wings were used to cover his face to prevent their viewing of God's glory. Therefore only two wings remained for service. So worship must forever take priority both quantitatively and qualitatively over duties.

An angelic category considered to be a symbol of heavenly things is called the cherubim. The initiatory reference to the Cherubim activities is found in Genesis 3:24 as they are standing guard, east of the Garden of Eden with a flaming sword which turned every way, to keep the way of the tree of life.

Then, in a very corroborative statement to the Cherubim mission of Divine justice, their figures are beaten of one piece of gold in the manufacture of the mercy seat in the tabernacle of the congregation with the cherubim messengers. As Divine agents of execution ready to strike at the slightest violation, the blood sprinkled redemptive application on the mercy seat became their only restraining influence since the precious blood reversed man's judgment of condemnation into a cleansing of forgiveness.

In Ezekiel 10 there is provided an astounding glimpse or pictures of the cherubim. In the passage, each Cherubim is presented as possessing, "four faces apiece and every one four wings; and the likeness of the hands of a man was under the wings." (Ezekiel 10:21). Not only did the cherubim possess wings and hands, but the keenness of vision for them was not a problematical issue since they were full of eyes.

A point of major practical, experiential and profound Theological discussions is the subject of cosmic powers when especially it is associated with the existence of demons. In every cultural setting from ancient times to the present, people have believed in the existence of demonic beings.

In antiquities past Neolithic surgeons in cases of epilepsy, insanity, or severe, or intractable headaches, would superstitiously insert holes in the head of the afflicted, erroneously believing that the holes provided an exit to allow the demon to vacate the premises. Then additionally, the afflicted extremist would adorn the surgically extracted bone disc, believing it would act as an amulet to prevent the demon's return.

The world of yesteryear was so dominated by poly-demonistic ideologies, that it seemed everyone had a notion or a potion. Plato identified demons with the souls of the dead and believed that they served as interpreters between gods and men. Aristotle believed in the popularized notion that all men have demons that follow them through life.

In Mesopotamia, demons were given names, since the Sumerians and the Babylonians believed in the magical power of names. They concurred that in exorcising a demon, his name must be used in a proper conjuration, or spell to ensure his exit.

Fear was forever instilled in a supernatural monomania of demonism consciousness. The Assyrians feared "Pazuzu," whom the Semitic world believed was the controller of creatures that caused every conceivable trouble. They also believed in "utukku," who were regarded as "devils" who lurked in the desert places to pounce upon the unwary sojourner.

Even among the Bible lands, demonic superstitions abounded as some believed that the empire of death was under two demons, one who ruled by day, and the other by night. Some also believed that gods should be worshipped at all times, but that demons should be worshipped at noon, or midday, conjecturing that the demons having been engaged all night, and rested at noon. Therefore, fear of the midday demon's ability to injure at that time of day was prevalently propagated. Some, therefore, believed that they must be appeased at that hour, without anyone waking them up. But God stated in Psalms 91:5 Thou shalt not be afraid for the terror by night, nor for the destruction that wasteth at the noonday

Even among the Greeks and Romans, there were outlandishly popular tales of polytheistic and polydemonistic conceptualizations. They believed that the very air itself was filled with evil spirits of all types. It, therefore, became their view that evil spirits were constantly attempting to invade humans and that the easiest method was to attach themselves to food before it was eaten? They, therefore, believed that food prior to consumption should be sacrificed to idols, in order to gain the god's favor, and also to cleanse the meat from demonic contamination.

Though Paul didn't indulge in the superstitious extremities of those before and after him, even so, he recognized the spiritual warfare existing between God's people and the devil, who was shooting "Flaming missiles" against the people of God. The "flaming missiles" (arrows) revealed the New Testament era warfare method of wrapping the tips of arrows to pieces of cloth that had been soaked in pitch. Then the arrow was ignited and on impact would spatter burning anything flammable, while also piercing and burning bodies.

In the days of Jesus, He constantly came in contact with "demons," with conclusively victorious results. The term demon in the New Testament is "daimon," which is also translated as devils in Matthew 8:31. Some linguistics experts believe that this term (daimon is most probably from a root word "da" meaning "a knowing one." In Jesus' day, man hypothesized that these invisible evil powers lived in unclean atmospheres and in deserts where there was no cleansing water and while originating the term "howling desert." They supposed that demons were particularly dangerous to travelers, newlyweds, women in childbirth, and also to children at nightfall.

It is concluded by many that demons are the disembodied spirits of the inhabitants of the pre-Adamite earth, whose sin instrumentalized the earthly ruination while destroying their bodies in themselves on the earth again.

The Bible veritably teaches that demons can cause dumbness (Matthew 9:32-33), blindness (Matthew 12:22), insanity (Luke 8), suicidal mania (Mark 9:22), and also can be the forces behind supernatural strength (Luke 8:29), and in some cases physical defects and deformities.

But with repetition in results Jesus defeated the demonic spirits, whether the opposition was the demoniac at the Capernaum synagogue, the two demoniacs at Gadara, or the Syrophenician's demonized daughter, nevertheless Jesus always prevailed.

In Ephesians 6, Paul refers to the believer conflict with demonic forces as we wrestle. The term wrestle reemployed in the passage was used of hand-to-hand combat, especially in the wrestling sphere of activity. To emphasize the serious nature of our encounter, wrestling in Paul's era, particularly in Rome, was characterized by trickery and deception, which possibly provided life for the winner, but death to the loser.

In this passage, Paul delineates the different strata or the ascendant rankings among the satanic network of demonic of subordinates, and hierarchy.

Paul refers to the rankings as principalities, powers, rulers of the darkness of this world, and spiritual wickedness in high places. The principalities category is the term "arche," meaning the beginning or government rule," and it has been used to describe the supramundane beings who exercise rule. It has also been described as the definition of angels and demons holding dominion entrusted to them in the order of things. Others believe that the term refers to angelic and demonic powers possessing political organization.

The strata of the demonic designated as "powers" are the Greek term "exousias" meaning authorities.

The term rulers of the darkness of this world is used in reference to the demonic classification defined as, "the world rulers of this darkness, or the rulers of this sinful world."

The category called "spiritual wickedness in high places" is described as "the spirit of wicked in the heavenlies," which some relate to the wicked spirits" that tempt men in their highest moments of spiritual fellowship.

Another category of major Theological interest in the study is the divine employment of "Angels as God's Agents in Judgments."

In 1 Chronicles chapter 21, there is revealed a setting of the angelic operation: in dispensing judgment. This occasion occurred as David erred when "Satan stood up against Israel and provoked David to number Israel." David's census in which he numbered his people was viewed by God as a demonstration of confidence of Judah, and the situation merited Divine retaliation. As a result, God sent judgment through an angel, which resulted in the loss of 70,000 men of Israel.

In ancient Egypt the religiously degenerate society engaged themselves in making the tombs of their dead more impregnable and lavish than their homes, believing that angelic would visit there in succeeding ages. The Egyptians were so supernaturally conscious that they even periodically fumigated" their temples and palaces from demonic infiltration, especially on the occasion of a funeral.

But during the era of Moses, as Pharaoh hardened his heart against God's command, God sent "an angel of death" that swept through Egypt killing all the first-born in every

Egyptian household. There was no Egyptian remedy of "fumigation" preventing this first-born destruction and only those under the blood of a (the) lamb, God's remedy was spared.

In Acts chapter 12, there is recorded a setting in which Josephus commentates was a festival honoring Claudius Caesar but the people of Sidon and Tyre, in danger of losing King Herod's favor and economic assistance, gave him worshipful adoration by stating, this is the voice of God and not man. Therefore an angel smote him, and Josephus recorded that he died five days later.

Another strategic incident of angelic judgmental execution transpired in the reign of Hezekiah King of Jerusalem, while the Assyrians threatened to attack Jerusalem. God, true to His prophetic promise relayed to Isaiah that not one Assyrian arrow would be fired into the city," And God sent an angel which dramatically destroyed 185,000 Assyrian soldiers.

In today's society, there is an indisputable awareness of the supernatural arena, or of the dimension that transcends physicality but has an unseen and influential reality.

Mankind, while seemingly unraveling emotionally, psychologically and spiritually has opened of his own volition, the door of his inner man "giving heed to seducing spirits and doctrines of devils, then speaking lies in hypocrisy while possessing a conscience seared with a hot iron" is highly characteristic of this age.

The term "seducing" spirits, reveals man's penchant for supernatural exploration and investigation, since "seducing" is the term "planes," or literally "wandering." It is interesting to note that "planos" is akin to "planao," which means "to cause to wander or to lead astray.

Man's gravitation to the "planao" seduction, has led him into Astrology, Numerology, Parapsychology and even "Dowsing", which refers to the search for and location of underground springs and other objects beneath the ground by using a divining rod. It is certainly a pathetic commentary on this age that some will look below, or beneath for satanic availability in search for divining water, when in reality they could look to God who provides. . . The Living Water, springing up into Everlasting Life".

Many times in this day of trouble it is easy to enter into sympathetic compassion with Paul's situation when he was, "Troubled on every side, yet not distressed; we are perplexed but not in despair; Persecuted but not destroyed "(II Cor. 4:8-9). The term trouble (thlibo) means "press," which metaphorically reveals Paul's heavy pressures, almost unbearable traumas, which made him feel like grapes put in a rock basin and then trampled underfoot by women and children. Paul's "distress" (stenochoreomai) means to be in a "narrow space," "to compress," or to be crushed. But regardless of the difficulties, though cast down (struck down) he was not destroyed (knocked out).

Possibly the vicissitude feelings of being in a winepress of crushing excruciation, or a narrow space equating to a proverbial tight squeeze may sum up Peter's view in prison while awaiting his execution. James, John's brother, had already faced the sword of execution, and now the magistrates in cooperation with hell were celebrating the ultimacy of Peter's destruction. But then an angel awakened Peter in the prison cell, causing the very chains of incarceration to lose their hold and Peter emerges from the supernaturally unlocked doors, following the angel to safety.

Elisha, the prophet, certainly faced the insurmountable encircling, or enveloping effect of trouble as the King of Syria dispatched his military troops to Dothan to dispose of the prophet who was intercepting the Syrian battle plans and thereby giving Israel counterattack plan advantages. As the prophet's helper naturally beheld their adversaries surrounding them, he exclaimed my master! How (what) shall we do? But strangely, Elisha declared, "Fear not: for they that be with us are more than they that be with them "(11 Kings 6:16). In modernistic language, Elisha was saying, "Don't be afraid... our army is bigger than theirs".

Then Elisha with great equipoise of calmness prayed that God would open the eyes of his servant. Then miraculously the veil of human visionary limitations was lifted, and the servant saw horses and chariots of fire surrounding Elisha.

Truly regardless of the magnitude of the dilemma the God that sent an angel, "to shut the lion's mouth, that sent 10,000 angels to descend upon Mount Sinai to confirm the Law of Moses, that David said possessed 20,000 angels passing through the celestial skyways, God has these angelic hosts as spectators in the cosmic and dispensational amphitheater of the world, but angels who instantaneously, can be Divinely dispatched as participators in the human arena are sent forth to minister to them that shall be heirs of salvation"

In James 2:19, The Apostle by that name states emphatically that "Thou believeth that there is ONE GOD; thou doest well; the devils also believe, and tremble.

The terms the devils tremble" oh yes it is just a remembrance of the Eternal Supremacy of the Almighty God that causes "the devils" to tremble, (Greek – "phrisso") or meaning to shudder with fear, yes extreme fear, and to be horrified with their eternal reservation in the Lake of Fire as the ultimate demonic destination.

The problem many times is that we are so explosively invaded by what we see, that we can't perceive the greater reality that GOD sees. But as GOD opened his servant's eyes that he knew that Elisha's adversaries had not incarcerated Elisha, but that GOD's Angelic arsenal had collected the "Celestial Advantage!!" Know this, when God lifts the blinds of humanistic visionary limitations for us to see only what HE Sees then the Man of God is no longer blind, or in a bind. 2 Corinthians 4:6 describes the problematical that prevents man from having the visionary acuity or clarity of perception to view spiritual realities with keenness. It states, In whom the god of this world hath blinded the minds of them which believe not, lest the light of the glorious gospel of Christ, who is The Image of God, should shine into them.

The term "god of this world," refers to the devil's captivating, or hypnotic delusionary influence that blinds the minds of the masses, while deceiving them into a lost mess of confusion in this age. The expression "hath blinded is the Greek word "typhloo" (toof-lo-0) which means to make blind, to darken the mind, or to obscure. It has been ascertained that this word is associated with the word "typhoon" and that our adversary that devil has caused a typhoon or major storm in the "mind's eye" of the unbeliever so that he can't see the things of GOD. Because Hell has caused a; typhoon, a cyclone, or a tsunami to becloud his potential to receive the Revelation of God, but anyone that knows GOD understands that HE IS IN COMMAND to AUTHORITATIVELY preside over Life's Demands. As Daniel 4:35 proudly elucidates, "And all the inhabitants of the earth are reputed as nothing: and He doeth according to (His will in Army of Heaven, and among the inhabitants of the earth: and none can stay His hand, or say unto Him, What doest thou?

In every human or spiritual warfare, none of that destructive stuff is Fair in Warfare, but God is the missing persuasion in every potential invasion that determines the outcome of victory.

Remember that Elijah was enormously outmanned 450-1 against the heathenistic false prophets of Baal, and he triumphantly prevailed. And 400 more false faces of idolatry were aligned with Asherah swelling the numbers against Elijah to 850-1, but Elijah was never done because The GOD of eternity had already won.

To graduate into higher levels of spiritual revelation we must stop looking at things from a superficial or external level of interpretation, and stop seeing what mankind sees with his limitations in practicality, and by Faith began to see what GOD sees in his eternal reality. "When we begin to see what GOD sees, only then can we see All that we can be because we will be introduced to GOD in HIS, eternal DYNAMICS of all things are possible to him that believeth.

In the Biblical history of the "Celestial Advantage," King Hezekiah, the 13th king of Judah, experienced Supernatural Angelic Interventions Angelic Intervention when Sennacherib the king of Assyria besieged Jerusalem with destructive intentionality.

But then GOD sent an angel and in one night destroyed 185,000 Assyrians. What a miracle! Because the Assyrian, along with their capital city inhabitants of Nineveh were historically notorious for their inhumane atrocities in their bloodthirsty treatment of foreigners.

They would flay, or peel the skin of their enemies, or impale them, by piercing them through with a penetrating pole and turning it into a spectator sport. They dismembered their prisoners and plucked out their tongues by the roots. An Assyrian monarch by the name of ASHURNASIRPAL 2nd boldly documented his mass executions by stating, "I slaughtered them, and with their blood, I dyed the mountains red like wool.

One of their demented kings celebrated because he erected a pyramid of heads in his city.

But Hezekiah, the son of Ahaz, whose name meant "Jehovah strengthens," put his Trust In The Lord!"

And Isaiah 37:36 miraculously and majestically reports, "...the angel of the Lord went forth, and smote in the camp of the Assyrians a hundred and fourscore five thousand: and when they arose early in the morning, behold, they were all dead corpses. So Sennacherib king of Assyria departed, and went, and returned, and dwelt at Nineveh. And it came to pass, as he was worshipping in the house of Nisrach his god that Adrammelech and Sarezer his sons smote him with the sword and they escaped into the land of Ararat and Esarhaddon his son reigned in his stead."

Therefore it is very strategic to know that THE JESUS CHRIST Salvation connection equals DIVINE PROTECTION. Remember this foundational Biblical fact of perpetual guaranteed security that Jesus revealed in St. Matthew 18:10 Take heed that ye despise not one of these little ones, for I say unto you, that in Heaven their angels do always behold the face of my father which is in Heaven.

As a father, a pastor, and a grandfather, I am forever 24-7 naming and claiming the promises of a GOD that will not and cannot lie. Just as Jesus blessed the little children, I believe in blessing them and invoking the promises of GOD to keep our children safe, and sound. We must regardless of the fluctuations of life recognize what the Apostle Paul declares in 2 Corinthians 1:20, "For all the promises of God in him are yea, and in him Amen, unto the Glory of God by us.

Even though JESUS took upon Him the form of a servant, and was made after the likeness of sinful flesh, at HIS discretion, HE could call on the armies of Heaven and place every earthly kingdom, domain, and regime in a fragile, predicament of vulnerability.

Know this that Hebrews 12:22 speaks of an "innumerable company of angels." And Revelation 5:11-12 reports that many angels, "numbering myriads of myriads, and thousands of thousands saying with a loud voice, Worthy is the lamb who was slain to receive power and wealth and wisdom and might and honor and glory and blessing!"

Please remember, yes capture the glory of this perpetual Holy Ghost believer's story, as Psalms 34:6-7 provides, "this poor man cried, and THE LORD heard him, and saved him out of all his troubles. And God did it, because "The angels of THE LORD encampeth round about them that fear HIM, and Delivereth them.

So climactically the JESUS name believer should never be intimidated, inhibited, or prohibited by anyone's status. Yes never be in a mindset of defeat, because the world thinks it's elite, because, in every board room, every classroom, every courtroom, God remains largely omnipotent, omniscient, omnipresent and in charge, and your angels stand with you in a GOD Ordained Connection for your protection.

Know this that, "we are not our own, and this earth is not our home." The Holy Spirit inspired believer is forever present in GOD'S Presence and everywhere he goes, his personally assigned angels travel also. And that is forever added to your advantage view that GOD'S Angels forever accompany you! Yes the celestial advantage!

Sources of Information

1. Angels, God's Secret Agents, Billy Graham, 1975, 1986
2. New Testament Words in Today's Language, Wayne A Detzler, 1986.
3. The MacArthur New Testament Commentary Hebrews, John MacArthur Jr., 1983
4. The Day Christ Died, Jim Bishop, 1957
5. Ludwig's Handbook of New Testament Rulers and Cities, Charles Ludwig. 1984
6. An Expository Dictionary of Biblical Words, W.E. Vine, 1985.
7. The MacArthur New Testament Commentary! Corinthians. John MacArthur Jr., 1984
8. The Reality of Angels, Lester Sumrall, 1982.
9. All the men of the Bible, Herbert Lockyer, 1985
10. The MacArthur New Testament Commentary Matthew 8-15, John MacArthur Jr., 1987
11. Christian Theology, Emery H. Bancroft, 1976.
12. The Word Bible Handbook, Lawrence O. Richards, 1982
13. Dispensational Truths, Clarence Larkin, 1920.
14. Rightly Dividing the Word, Clarence Larkin, 1920
15. The MacArthur New Testament Commentary Ephesians, John MacArthur Jr., 1986
16. Dictionary of Biblical Literacy, Cecil B. Murphey, 1989
17. The Thompson Chain-Reference Bible, Charles F. Thompson, 1982.

18. The Ultimate Priority On Worship, John MacArthur Jr., 1983

19. The Tabernacle Camping With God, Stephen F. Olford, 1971

20. The Bible and Modern Medicine, A Rendle Short, 1953

21. The Pictorial Encyclopedia of the Bible, 195-1976

22. Clarke's Commentary, Adam Clarke, date unknown

23. The Miracles of Jesus, Leslie B. Flynn, 1990

24. Word Meanings in the New Testament, Ralph Earle, 1986.

25. Be Dynamic, Warren W. Wiersbe, 1987

26. The Internet